PIANO Adventures® by Nancy and Randall Faber
A BASIC PIANO METHOD

LESSON BOOK

Production: Frank and Gail Hackinson
Production Coordinator: Marilyn Cole
Editors: Victoria McArthur and Edwin McLean
Cover and Illustrations: Gwen Terpstra Design, San Francisco
Engraving: GrayBear Music Company, Hollywood, Florida
Printer: Trend Graphics

CONTENTS

The student or teacher may wish to put a ✓ or date in the blank to show when a piece has been completed.

Review

| | Review Test: rhythm, reading, theory, symbols and terms | 4 |
| | Review Piece, *Maple Leaf Rag*, ♪ ♩ ♪ | 6 |

UNIT 1 — Sixteenth Notes

	Introduction of 16th notes, Drummer at the Keyboard	8
	Little Joke, ♩♬ rhythm	9
	Burlesca, pattern and sequence, L.H. broken octaves, CREATIVE	10
	Bridal March, ♩.♪ rhythm	12
	The Gondola, 16th notes in 6/8 time, *cantabile*	14

UNIT 2 — Chord Inversions

	Theory of Chord Inversions	16
	Table of Chord Inversions	17
	Sonatina in C, analysis	18

Seaside Suite:

	Sailboats in the Wind, 1st inversion chords, grace note	21
	Mysterious Cove, trill, CREATIVE	24
	Surfboards, 2nd inversion chords	26

UNIT 3 — minor scales

Minor Scales

Theory of the Natural and Harmonic Minor Scales	28
Playing Natural and Harmonic Minor Scales: Am, Dm, Em	29
In the Hall of the Mountain King, **sfz**	30
The V7 Chord in Root Position	32
Prelude in D Minor, tonic and dominant 7th chords in Dm	33
Night Ride, major/minor key signatures	34
The Sailor's Story, tonic and dominant 7th chords in Em, adagio	36
Chanson, relative major and minor review, CREATIVE	37

UNIT 4 — 2 octave scales

Two-Octave Scales

Sharp Key Signatures, writing the sharp pattern	40
Playing Two-Octave Scales, C, G, D, A, E, B	40
Wild Flowers, Key of A major, *molto*	42
Procession, Key of E major, *poco a poco*	44

Special Achievement Piece

Prelude in C, J.S. Bach (WTC Book 1, No. 1)	45

Certificate of Achievement	48

Note: The pieces in this book are by Nancy Faber unless otherwise indicated.

Review Test

Rhythm

1. Match the symbols to the correct terms with a connecting line.

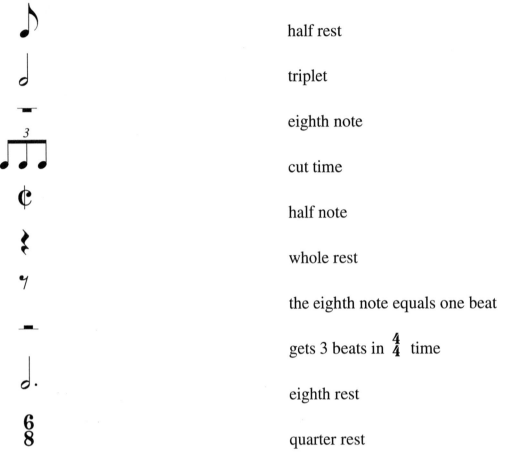

half rest

triplet

eighth note

cut time

half note

whole rest

the eighth note equals one beat

gets 3 beats in $\frac{4}{4}$ time

eighth rest

quarter rest

2. Fill in the blanks below.

Ritardando means to _____

The term *a tempo* means _____

This upbeat begins on beat ____ .

Fermata 🠉 means _____

Reading

3. Name the following intervals: (2nd, 3rd, 4th, 5th, 6th, 7th)

4. Name these key signatures.

Key of ____

Key of ____

Key of ____

Theory

5. Circle the correct key from the X.

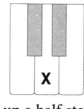 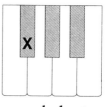

up a half step   up a whole step

6. Add the correct sharps or flats to complete each scale.

G major scale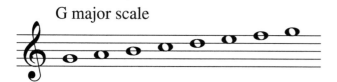

F major scale

D major scale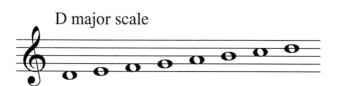

Chromatic scale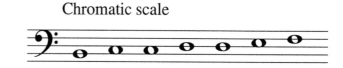

7. Label these chords correctly as **I**, **IV**, or **V7**.

Key of G   Key of D   Key of F   Key of C

 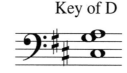  

_____   _____   _____   _____

Symbols & Terms

8. Put these dynamic marks in order from softest to loudest.

f *ff* *mp* *mf* *p* *pp*

softest   loudest

9. Fill in the blanks below.

Draw a sharp ____, a flat ____, a natural ____

Allegro means _____

Andante means _____

Vivace means _____

Moderato means _____

10. Under each note draw:

an accent mark: tenuto (stress) mark: staccato mark:

Review Piece

Tap this rhythm from *Maple Leaf Rag* with both hands. Your teacher may ask you to count aloud. (Notice each beat is divided into 2 equal parts.)

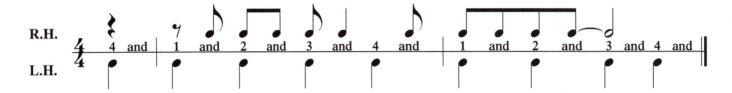

Practice Hints:

1. First tap the whole piece hands together at a slow tempo.
2. Play hands separately noticing the fingering and dynamics.
3. Now play hands together, gradually working up to performance speed.

Maple Leaf Rag

Scott Joplin
(1868-1917, U.S.A.)
arranged

 Point out the following in this piece:

eighth rest   accidental   V7 chord   6th

UNIT 1

16th Notes

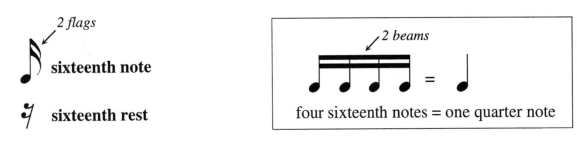

With your teacher, tap and count aloud the rhythm below. Notice each beat is divided into 4 equal parts: **1 e and a**

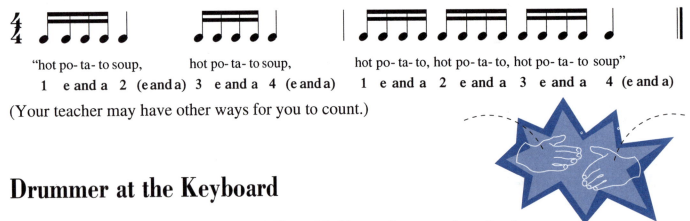

"hot po- ta- to soup,   hot po- ta- to soup,   hot po- ta- to, hot po- ta- to, hot po- ta- to soup"
   1 e and a 2 (e and a) 3 e and a 4 (e and a)   1 e and a 2 e and a 3 e and a 4 (e and a)

(Your teacher may have other ways for you to count.)

Drummer at the Keyboard

On the closed keyboard lid, tap your R.H. and L.H. together counting aloud.
Practice this drill until you can do it with ease. Can you tap with the metronome at ♩ = 72?

Little Joke
(Op. 39, No. 12)

As you play *Little Joke*, drop into beat 1 of each measure.
Play the right hand eighth notes with a crisp, staccato touch.

Dmitri Kabalevsky
(1904-1987, Russia)
original form

DISCOVERY

Play the L.H. alone as blocked chords. Then play the R.H. alone as blocked chords.
Can you play hands together using blocked chords?

Sequence

A short musical pattern that is repeated on another pitch is called a *sequence*.

Play:

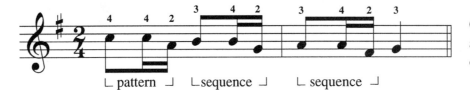

Can you make up a pattern and sequence of your own?

Practice Hints:

1. Play *Burlesca* with the right hand alone, noticing the patterns and sequences.

2. The left hand uses broken octaves. Practice the L.H. alone slowly, keeping a relaxed wrist. Shift your hand slightly to help reach the octave.

3. Now play hands together, gradually working up to performance speed.

Burlesca*

(from Notebook for Wolfgang)

Review: *Allegretto* means cheerful and rather fast (but not as fast as *Allegro*).

Leopold Mozart
(1719-1787, Austria)
original form

*A *burlesca* is a composition with a lively, playful character.
  Leopold Mozart wrote this piece while teaching his son, the famous Wolfgang Amadeus Mozart.

Compose your own pattern followed by 3 sequences.
Call it "Mountain Climbing" or a title of your choice.

Extra Credit: Can you transpose the first 8 measures of *Burlesca* to the Key of C?
Reading the intervals and using your "ear" will help you transpose.

The ♩.♪ rhythm is used in many marches. This familiar wedding march will help you master this common dotted rhythm.

Bridal March

(from the opera *Lohengrin*)

Richard Wagner
(1813-1883, Germany)
arranged

DISCOVERY

The ♩.♪ rhythm in this piece always occurs on:
beat 1   *beat 2*   (circle one)

Review: **6/8** = 6 beats in a measure / ♪ gets 1 beat

The Gondola

Success Hint: Learn this piece hands separately before playing hands together.

The Italian word cantabile is pronounced, "con-TAH-bee-lay."

DISCOVERY

In $\frac{6}{8}$ time, how many beats does each rhythm below receive?

♩. ♩ = ___ beats   ♩. ♪ = ___ beats   ♩. ♩. = ___ beats

UNIT 2

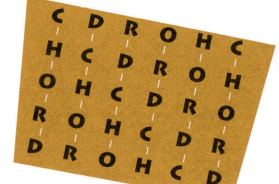

Chord Inversions

1. Major and minor chords are composed of a **root, 3rd,** and **5th.**
   These notes can be rearranged, or **inverted** to form **chord inversions.**

   To invert a chord, bring the lowest tone up an octave.

   C major chord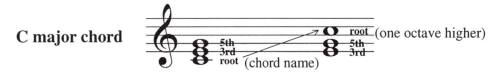

   The letter names stay the same, even though the notes are rearranged.

2. **Major and minor chords have three positions: root position, 1st inversion, and 2nd inversion.**
   Play the following positions of the C major chord. Notice the fingering.

   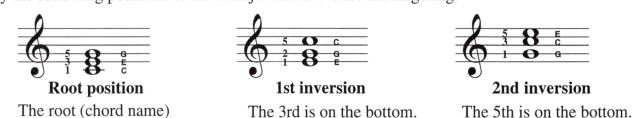

   Root position   **1st inversion**   **2nd inversion**
   The root (chord name)   The 3rd is on the bottom.   The 5th is on the bottom.
   is on the bottom.

3. **To find the root (chord name) of a chord inversion:**
   Locate the interval of a 4th in the inversion.
   The root will always be the *upper* note of the 4th.

   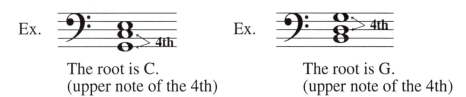

   The root is C.   The root is G.
   (upper note of the 4th)   (upper note of the 4th)

4. For each chord below, darken the interval of a 4th.
   Then write the name of the root (chord name) in the blank.

   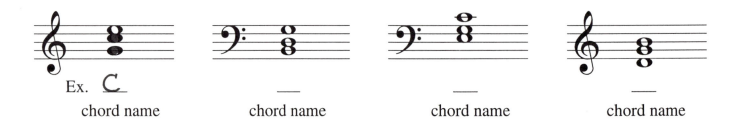

   Ex. C   ___   ___   ___
   chord name   chord name   chord name   chord name

Table of Chord Inversions

Put a check (✓) in the box as you master the following chord inversions at a moderate tempo.

❏ **C major chords**

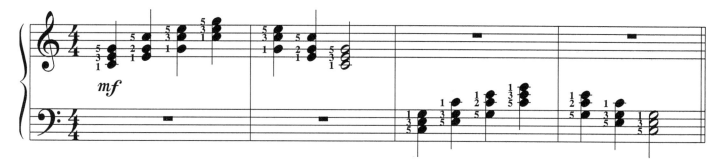

❏ **F major chords**

❏ **G major chords**

❏ **D major chords**

Your teacher may ask you to play the exercise above using the following chords.
(You may proceed in the book while practicing these chords.)

1. ❏ **A minor**   2. ❏ **D minor**   3. ❏ **E minor**   4. ❏ **C minor**
5. ❏ **G minor**   6. ❏ **F minor**   7. ❏ **A major**   8. ❏ **E major**

Analyzing a piece (studying the patterns) can help you learn and memorize the music quickly.

Analyze this piece with your teacher before playing hands together.

Sonatina in C

Discovery: What inversion of the C major chord is used for the R.H. in measures 37-40? _____

Extra Credit: Can you transpose the Coda to the Key of G?

Grace note

A *grace note* is an ornamental note that has no time value of its own.
It is played quickly into the note that follows.
Your teacher will show you how to play the grace notes in the last measures.

A *suite* is a set of pieces that are usually performed together. A suite is often a collection of dances, or may be a set of pieces that share a common idea. *Seaside Suite* depicts a day at the seashore.

The first movement, *Sailboats in the Wind*, uses **1st inversion chords** for the right hand.

Practice Hint: First play the broken chords as blocked chords.
This will help you recognize chord names and patterns.

Seaside Suite

1. Sailboats in the Wind

Theory p. 14, 15

DISCOVERY Find a two-measure pattern and sequence for the L.H. on p. 22.

23

trill (*tr*) - a rapid alternation between two neighboring notes.
Your teacher will show you how to play the trill in the last measure.

2. Mysterious Cove

Hold the pedal down and play a low G in the L.H.
For the R.H., play *1st inversion chords* using only white keys.

This last movement uses **2nd inversion chords** for the R.H.

Keeping your hand in a relaxed, but molded playing position will help you play the consecutive 2nd inversion chords.

3. Surfboards

*Delete lower note of octaves, if necessary.

DISCOVERY
Name the root of the 1st four R.H. chords. (Hint: Remember to look for the upper note of each 4th.) Is each chord major or minor?

Theory of Minor Scales

- Every major key also has a minor key that shares the **same key signature.**
  The minor key is called the **relative minor.**

- The relative minor starts on the **6th step** of the major scale.
  Hint: You can also find it quickly by counting down 3 half steps from the tonic of the major key.

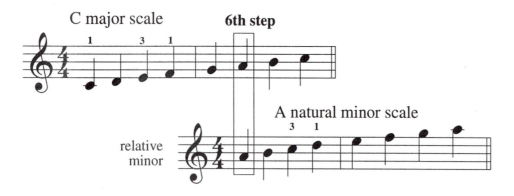

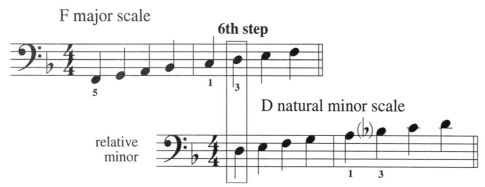

Play these two major scales and their relative minors. Listen to the difference in sound!

The Harmonic Minor Scale

- The minor scales shown above are called **natural minor** scales.
  Notice the **whole step** between steps 7 and 8 in the natural minor scale.

- The **harmonic minor** scale is formed by **raising the 7th step** of the natural minor scale.
  This creates a **half step** between steps 7 and 8 (*leading tone* to *tonic*).
  Notice an accidental is needed to raise the 7th step.

Play the A harmonic minor scale and listen to the sound!

Playing Minor Scales

Practice these minor scales listening for an even tone and steady rhythm.
Put a ✓ in the box when you have mastered the metronome speeds your teacher suggests.

❏ 1st week ♩ = _____   ❏ 2nd week ♩ = _____   ❏ 3rd week ♩ = _____

Teacher note: The student may proceed in the book while developing speed on these scales.

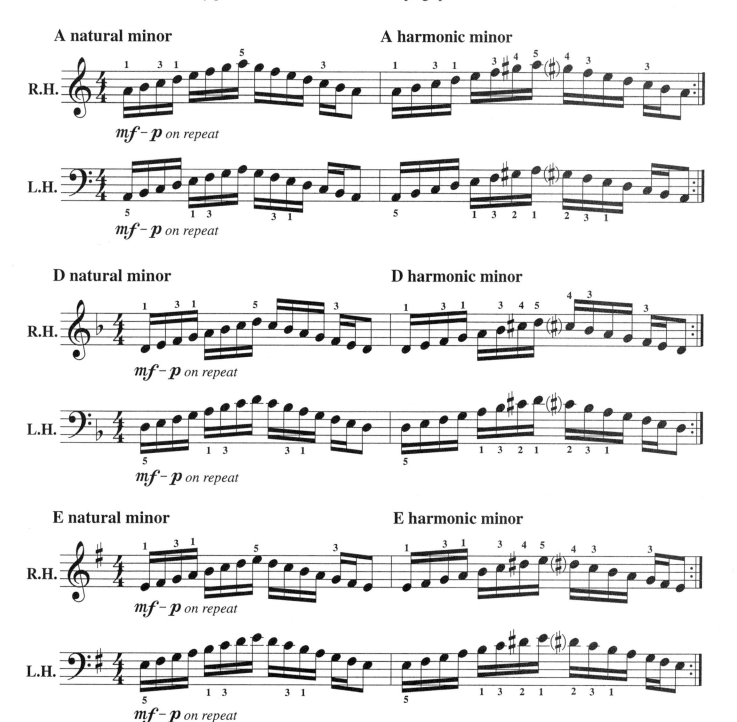

Note to Teacher: The student may continue learning all 12 harmonic minor scales with *Achievement Skill Sheet No. 4*, One-Octave Minor Scales & Arpeggios.

sfz – *sforzando*

A sudden, strong accent on a single note or chord.

In the Hall of the Mountain King

(from *Peer Gynt Suite*)

Edvard Grieg
(1843-1907, Norway)
arranged

Crisp march tempo (♩ = 100-120)

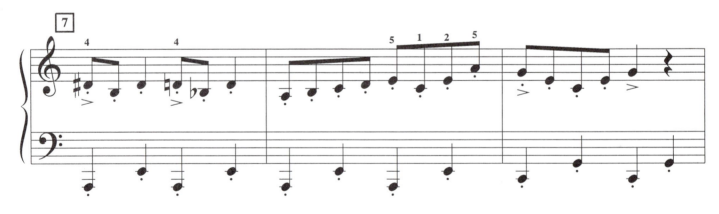

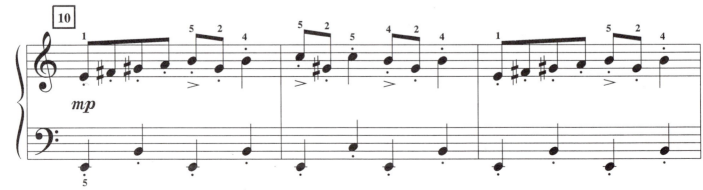

DISCOVERY
Does the G♯ in the last measure belong to the A natural minor scale or the A harmonic minor scale? _____

Extra Credit: Can you transpose measures 2-9 to D minor?

The V⁷ Chord in Root Position

Review: Tonic refers to **step 1** of the scale. Dominant refers to **step 5** of the scale.

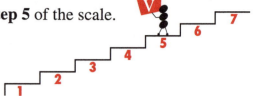

1. **Playing the V Chord in Root Position**

   The dominant chord is always a **major chord** built on **step 5** of the scale.
   It is also called the V (five) chord.

   In the keys shown below, play and say the following:

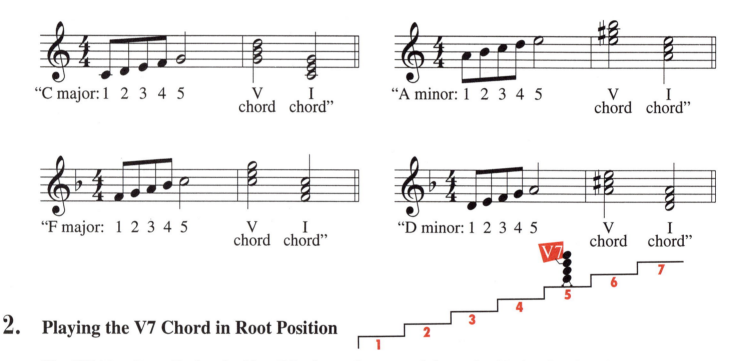

2. **Playing the V7 Chord in Root Position**

   The **V7** (dominant 7) chord adds a **7th above the root** of the major V chord. It is a four-note chord.
   Often, one of the middle notes is omitted, making it easier to play.

   In the keys shown below, play and say the following:

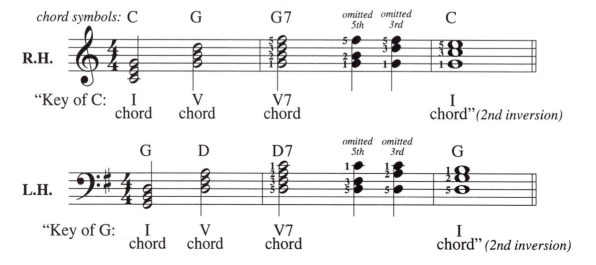

32

I and V7 Chords in D minor (root position)

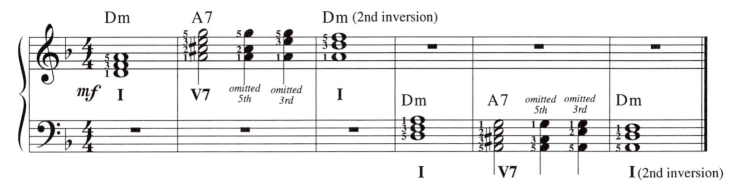

Prelude in D Minor

(from Op. 43)

Practice Hint: Play this piece slowly in 4/4 time, gradually working up to performance tempo in cut time.

Muzio Clementi
(1752-1832, Italy)
original form

Naming Key Signatures

A key signature indicates a major key or the relative minor key.
For example, the key signature of *Night Ride* is either F major or D minor.
To determine the correct key, look at the harmony in the last measure.

Look at the last measure of *Night Ride,* then name the key.   **Key of** _____

Technique Hints:

1. Practice the R.H. with a loose, relaxed wrist.
   Play lightly and close to the keys.

2. Practice the L.H. with a rich tone, "shaping" each phrase.

Night Ride

Key of _____ **minor**

Cornelius Gurlitt
(1843-1907, Germany)
original form

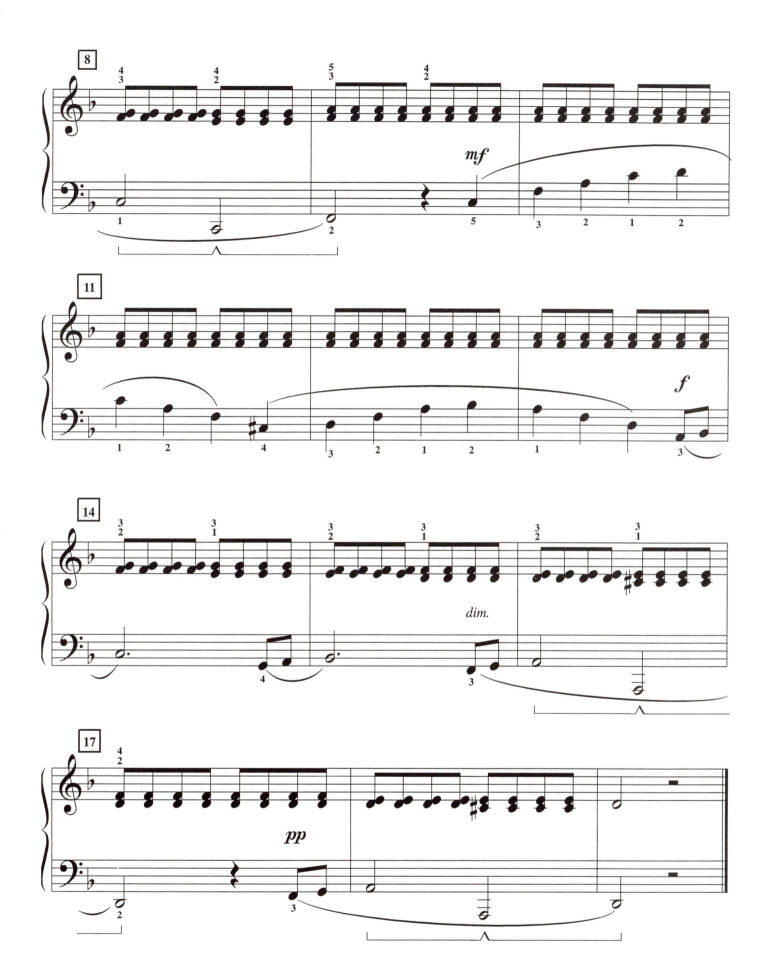

DISCOVERY

In measures 8-11 this piece moves to F major.
In what measure does the leading tone appear, returning the piece to D minor? *measure* ___

Sometimes a composer uses the major key and its relative minor key in the same piece.

Name the form of the piece and the key used for each section. _____ _____
                                                                                form   keys

Chanson*

Technique Hint: Play the L.H. alone with pedal. Keep your wrist in motion as your hand moves gracefully through the wide leaps.

Chanson is the French word for "song."

Compose a 4-measure melody in G major.
Can you play your melody in the relative minor (E minor)?

Sharp Key Signatures

UNIT 4 — 2 octave scales

To name a key signature with sharps, follow this rule:

Go up a half step from the **last sharp** in the key signature.

The name of that note is the name of the key.
(Hint: The last sharp in the key signature is the *leading tone* of the key.)

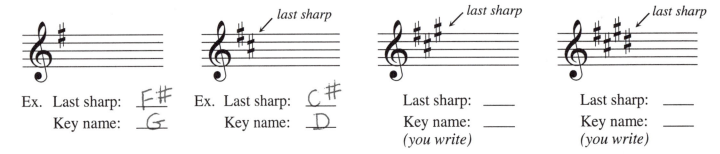

Ex. Last sharp: F#
Key name: G

Ex. Last sharp: C#
Key name: D

Last sharp: ___
Key name: ___
(you write)

Last sharp: ___
Key name: ___
(you write)

The pattern of sharps is always the same.
Study the example below and the rules to the right.
Then write 2 complete sharp patterns on your own.

1. Always begin with F#.
2. Continue the pattern moving **down a 4th** and **up a 5th**.
3. After the fourth sharp, D#, move **down** to A#. Then continue the "up 5, down 4" pattern.

F# C# G# D# A# E# B#

(you write)   *(you write)*

1. Two-Octave Scales

Practice these scales **hands separately**. Use *cresc.* and *dim.* to add "shape" to the scale.
Put a ✓ or date in the blanks below as each tempo is mastered.

C major

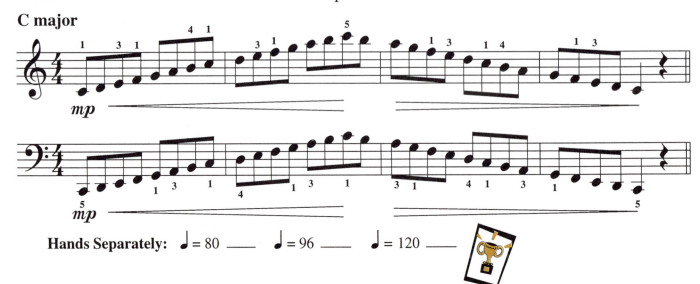

Hands Separately: ♩ = 80 ___   ♩ = 96 ___   ♩ = 120 ___

40

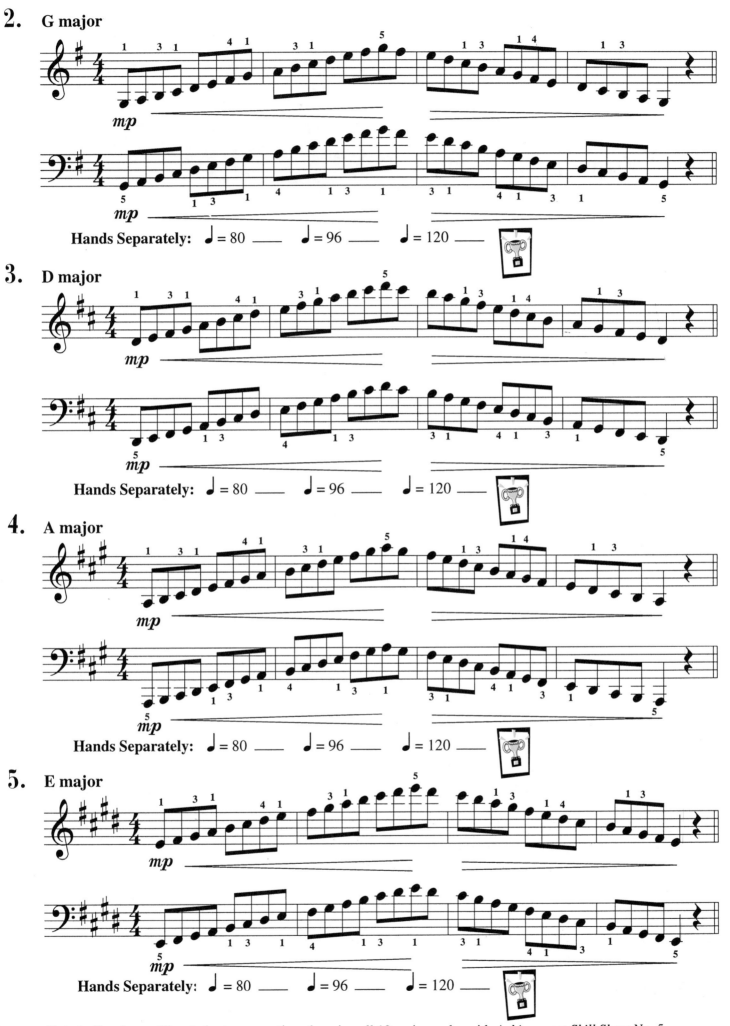

2. G major

3. D major

4. A major

5. E major

Hands Separately: ♩ = 80 ___ ♩ = 96 ___ ♩ = 120 ___

Note to Teacher: The student may continue learning all 12 major scales with *Achievement Skill Sheet No. 5. Two Octave Major Scales & Arpeggios.*

Molto means "very."
For example, *molto rit.* means to make a very big *ritardando*.

Wild Flowers

DISCOVERY

How many times does the opening theme appear?

Poco a poco means "little by little."
For example, *cresc. poco a poco* means to get louder, little by little.

Procession

Key of _____ Major

DISCOVERY

Does the opening chord have the root, 3rd, or 5th on top (as the melody)? _____
Does the last chord have the root, 3rd, or 5th on top? _____

This prelude is one of Johann Sebastian Bach's most well-loved keyboard pieces. Bach was a master at creating an entire composition from a single musical idea.

Bach's original manuscript did not include dynamic marks. The dynamic marks given here show one interpretation for the piece. Your teacher may suggest other dynamic marks for you to play.

Congratulations on being able to play this advanced piece from the keyboard repertoire!*

Prelude in C

(No. 1 from *The Well-Tempered Clavier,* Book 1)

Johann Sebastian Bach
(1685-1750, Germany)
original form

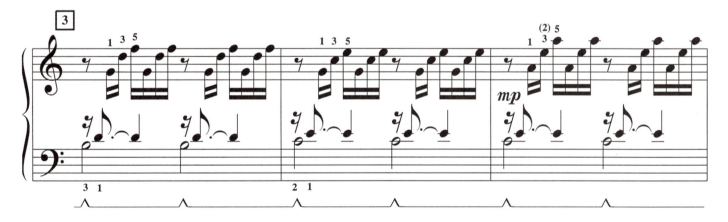

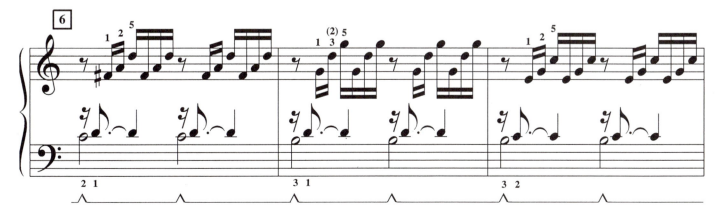

*As a pianist, your *repertoire* is the collection of pieces you can play at performance level.

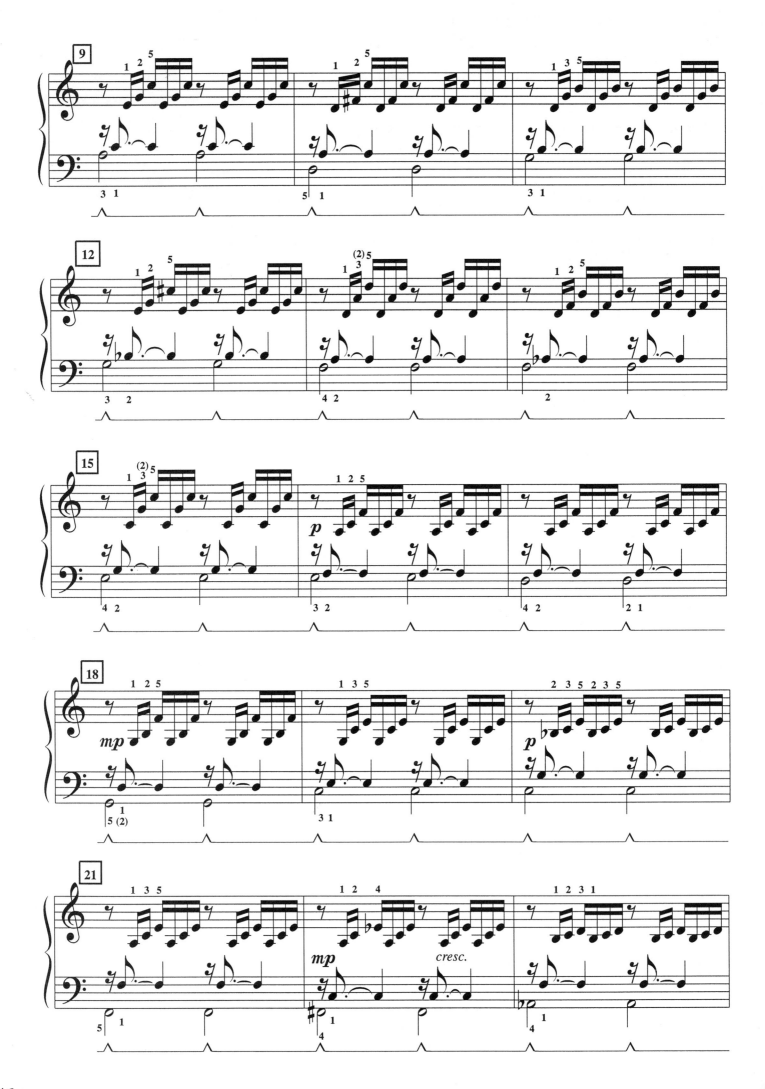

DISCOVERY
Where does the L.H. bass note stay on the dominant for 8 consecutive measures?

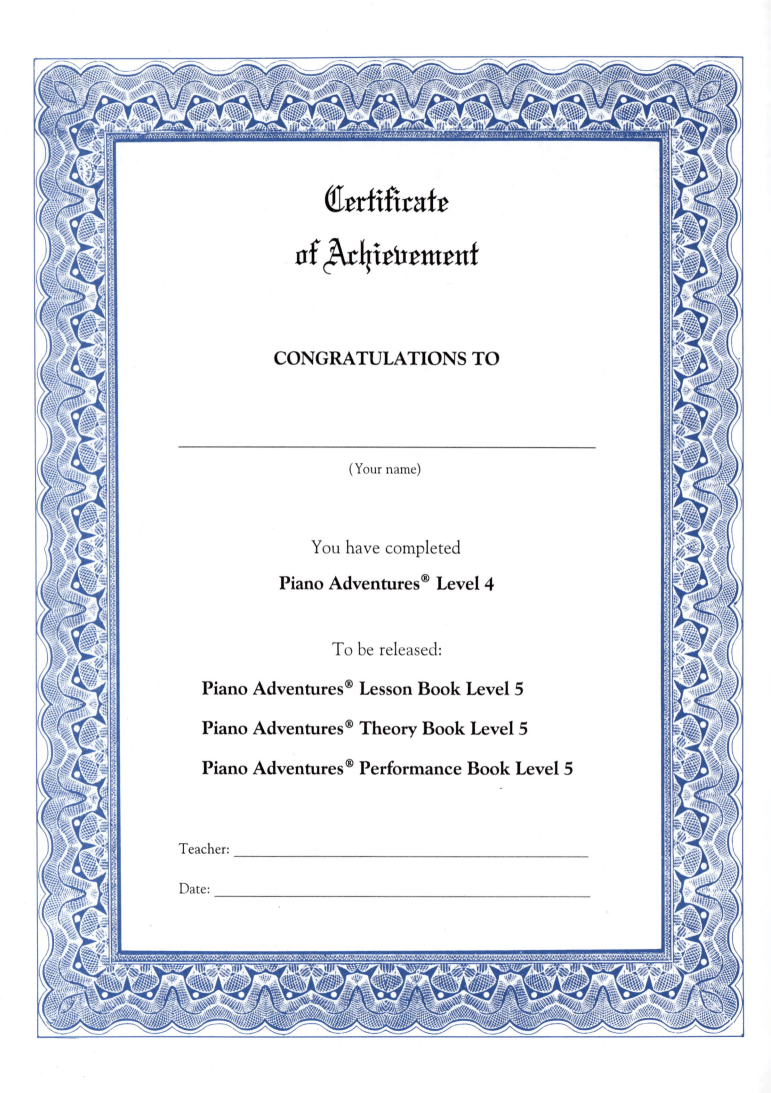